From Your Friends At **The MAILBOX®**

DECEMBER

A MONTH OF REPRODUCIBLES AT YOUR FINGERTIPS!

Kindergarten

Project Editor:
Angie Kutzer

Contributing Editors:
Ada Goren, Allison E. Ward

Writers:
Joe Appleton, Susan Bunyan, Susan Deriso,
Rhonda Dominguez, Henry Fergus, Diane Gilliam,
Lucia Kemp Henry, Kathleen Padilla, Kelli Plaxco

Art Coordinator:
Clevell Harris

Artists:
Jennifer Tipton Bennett, Cathy Spangler Bruce,
Clevell Harris, Lucia Kemp Henry, Susan Hodnett,
Rob Mayworth, Rebecca Saunders, Donna K. Teal

Cover Artist:
Jennifer Tipton Bennett

©1999 by THE EDUCATION CENTER, INC.
All rights reserved.
ISBN #1-56234-274-6

Manufactured in the United States

10 9 8 7 6 5 4 3 2 1

Table Of Contents

BOOKS TO CHECK OUT:

TO DO:

BIRTHDAYS:

MEETINGS:

SPECIAL DATES:

DUTIES THIS MONTH:

DECEMBER CLASSROOM THEMES:

MATERIALS TO COLLECT:

DECEMBER

Ridin' The Rails

All aboard! It's time for some reproducible activities that are just perfect for enhancing a unit on trains.

Choo-Choo Review

Capitalize on youngsters' eager anticipation of the winter holidays with this circle-time idea. To prepare, duplicate the patterns on page 7. Color the patterns and cut them out. Glue the North Pole picture to the top right-hand corner of a large sheet of poster board. Draw a curvy set of train tracks leading from the lower left corner of the poster board to the North Pole. Make the number of spaces between rails equal to the number of school days you have in December. Glue the "Whistle Stop" signs along the track, wherever you desire. Program each space in the train track with a different task. (See the illustration for examples.) Then laminate the poster board and the train pattern.

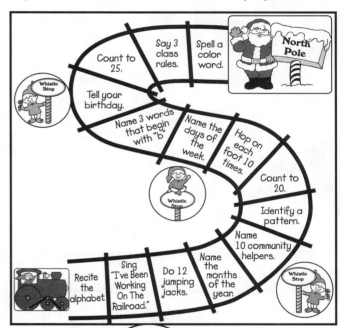

On the first school day in December, place the train on the track's first space (using a bit of Sticky-Tac). Ask youngsters to perform the task written in that space during circle time. Continue each day, moving the train along the track. When you come to a "Whistle Stop," take time out for a treat, such as a special snack, a few extra minutes on the playground, or a No-Nap Day. Keep going until you reach the North Pole and a well-deserved winter break!

Keep basic-skills review on the right track with the reproducibles on pages 8 and 9.

NORTH POLE

5

"I Can!"

Looking for good literature about locomotives? Share the classic *The Little Engine That Could™* by Watty Piper (Platt & Munk, Publishers). Discuss with your students the determination and diligence the Little Blue Engine displayed when crossing the mountain for the first time. Invite your little learners to brainstorm a list of things *they* can do now that they've reached the midpoint of the school year. Give each child a copy of page 10. Demonstrate how to cut out the large rectangle on the heavy lines, then carefully match the corners and fold on the lighter lines (lengthwise first) to create a booklet. Have each youngster write her name on the cover, then dictate and illustrate one thing she can do on each of her booklet's three pages. Invite each child to share her booklet with a partner.

On A Train Ride

Another great railroad read-aloud is *The Train Ride* by June Crebbin (Candlewick Press). After sharing this story with your class, duplicate the creative-writing sheet on page 11 for each student. Ask each child to illustrate what he might see if he went on a train ride. Take his dictation or have him use invented spelling to write a description of his picture in the blank.
Lots of creativity—that's what *you'll* see!

Railroad-Crossing Crunchies

If heading down the track has your students hungry for a snack, provide the ingredients for this railroad-related treat. Set up a snack station with a class supply of paper plates and plastic knives, one English muffin half per child, yellow-tinted cream cheese, pretzel sticks, and a couple of tubes of brown or black gel icing. Duplicate a class supply of page 12. Invite each child to visit the station and assemble her snack by following the directions on her reproducible.

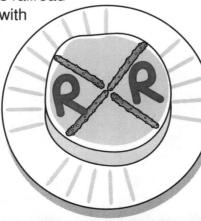

Name _____

Down To The Station

Follow the alphabet.

©1999 The Education Center, Inc. • *December Monthly Reproducibles* • Kindergarten • TEC967

Name _____

Boxcar Counting

✂ Cut out the numbers.

🧴 Glue them in order.

North Pole

2	10	18	25
1	9	17	
7	15	23	
	14		
		21	
4			
	11	19	

| 22 | 5 | 24 | 13 | 8 | 20 | 6 | 12 | 3 | 16 |

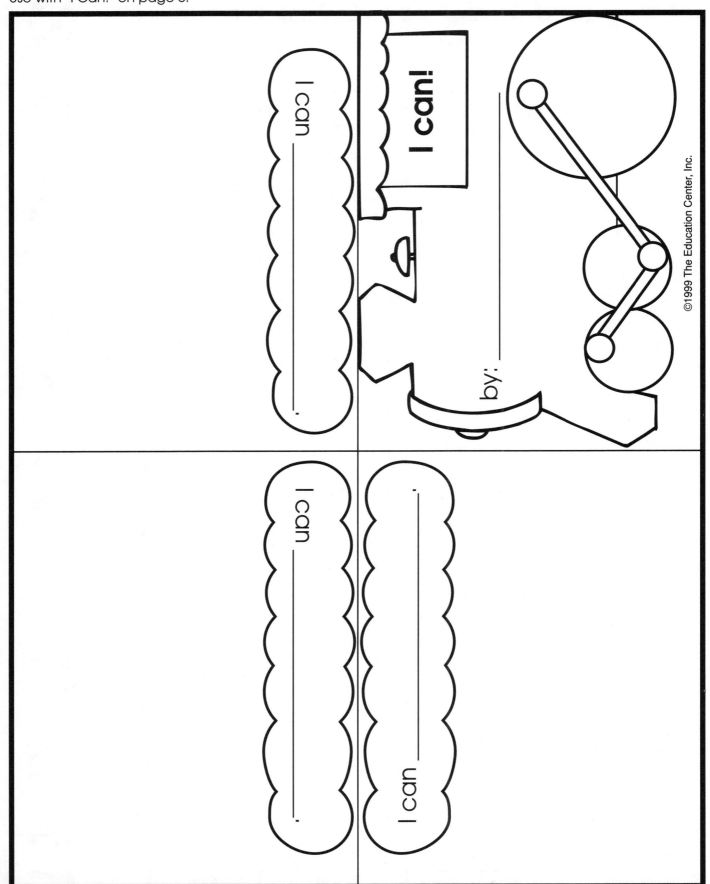

What A Trip!

If I went on a train ride, I might see
_____.

Railroad-Crossing Crunchie

You will need:

 1 paper plate

 1 plastic knife

 1 English muffin half

 pretzel sticks

 yellow cream cheese

 gel icing

 Spread cream cheese on the muffin.

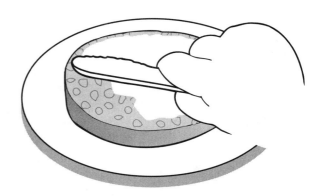

 Arrange the pretzel sticks.

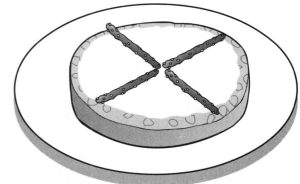

 Draw two *R*s.

Happy Hanukkah

Use these fun, skill-building ideas to make the Festival of Lights the highlight of December!

Eight Is Great!

Hanukkah lasts for eight nights. Locate the beginning of Hanukkah on your classroom calendar; then count and mark the eight nights. Explain that many Jewish youngsters receive gifts on each of these eight nights. Give a copy of page 15 to each child; then invite her to read the color word on each gift and color it with the corresponding crayon. How festive!

Spin The Dreidel

A game of dreidel is not just fun—it's great math practice, too! If your youngsters aren't familiar with how to play, teach them. Provide a commercial or homemade dreidel, and use nuts, pennies, or any kind of counters you have handy. For more math practice, follow up the game by giving a copy of page 16 to each student. Encourage each child to count the dot sets on each dreidel, then write the corresponding numeral in the space provided.

Hanukkah Greetings

It's traditional for Jewish children to receive *gelt* at Hanukkah. Gelt is money, and it is usually given in the form of coins. Sometimes children receive gold foil–wrapped chocolate coins instead of real coins at Hanukkah. Invite your youngsters to practice this tradition with the greeting card on page 17. Duplicate a class supply of the patterns on page 17 onto white construction paper. Have each child follow these directions:

1. Cut out the dreidel pattern and fold it as indicated.
2. Cut out the greeting boxes and glue them in place on the front of the folded card.
3. Write (or dictate) the recipient's name at the top of the dreidel.
4. Sign your name at the bottom.
5. Use a gold glitter crayon to color the gold coins on the inside of the card.

If desired, provide gold foil–wrapped chocolate coins and envelopes. Have each child tuck a chocolate coin inside her folded card; then have her slip the card into an envelope and address it to the recipient. Happy Hanukkah!

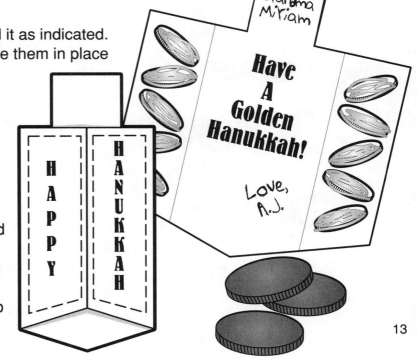

13

Menorah Math

The central symbol of Hanukkah is the *menorah,* which holds one candle to represent each of the eight nights of Hanukkah, plus the *shammash,* a helper candle used to light all the others. Show your students a real menorah or a picture of one. Explain that the candles are inserted into the menorah from right to left, but are lit from left to right.

Use the symbol of the menorah to practice patterning skills. Give a copy of page 18 to each child. Invite him to color the candles in each menorah, creating a different color pattern on each one.

For numeral-matching practice, create a center game with the reproducible on page 19. Duplicate onto tagboard enough copies of page 19 for small-group use. Color and cut apart the candles at the bottom of each copy; then laminate the candles and menorah mats. Make a spinner with eight sections as shown. To play, each child takes a turn spinning the spinner, and then putting the candle with the corresponding numeral into his menorah. The first player to fill his menorah wins. Once students are familiar with the game, add the challenge that the candles must go into each menorah in numerical order.

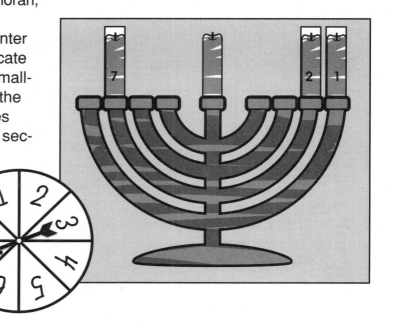

L Is For Latkes

One of the tastiest traditions of Hanukkah is the eating of *latkes*—potato pancakes. Use this vocabulary word to teach the sound of *L.* Duplicate the latke patterns on page 20 onto tagboard; then cut them out. Write the letter "L" on the back of each latke that shows a picture of something beginning with the sound of *L.* If desired, laminate the pieces for durability. Put the latkes, a frying pan, and a spatula in a center. Invite two children at a time to visit the center. One child lays all the latkes picture-side-up on a tabletop. He chooses the latkes that begin with the sound of *L* and places them—still picture-side-up—in the pan to "fry." His partner then uses the spatula to remove each latke and flip it back onto the tabletop, checking for the "L" on the back to make sure his partner chose correctly. Ready? Let's fry and flip!

Eight Colorful Gifts

 Color.

red

orange

purple

blue

white

green

black

yellow

15

Dotted Dreidels

Name_____

Count.

Write.

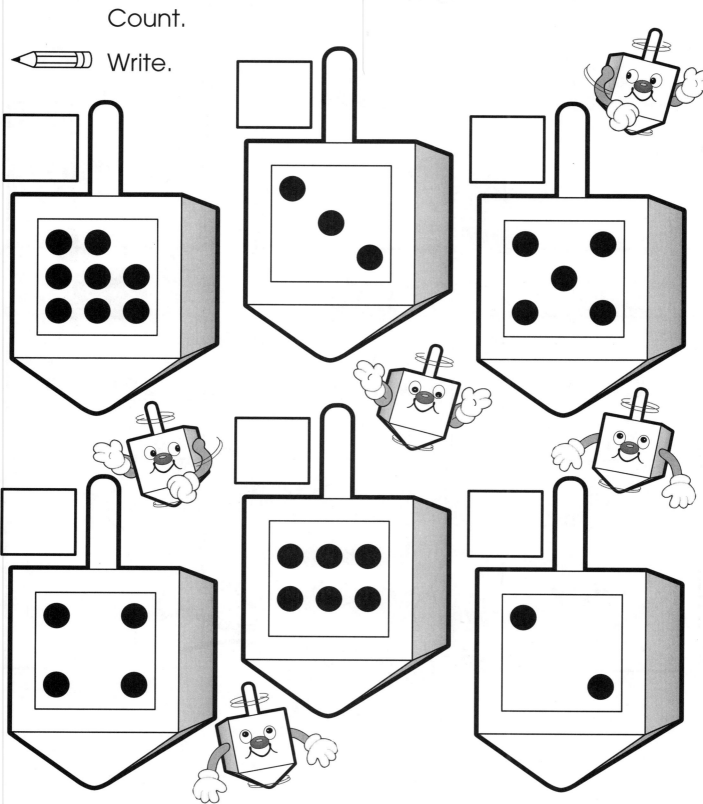

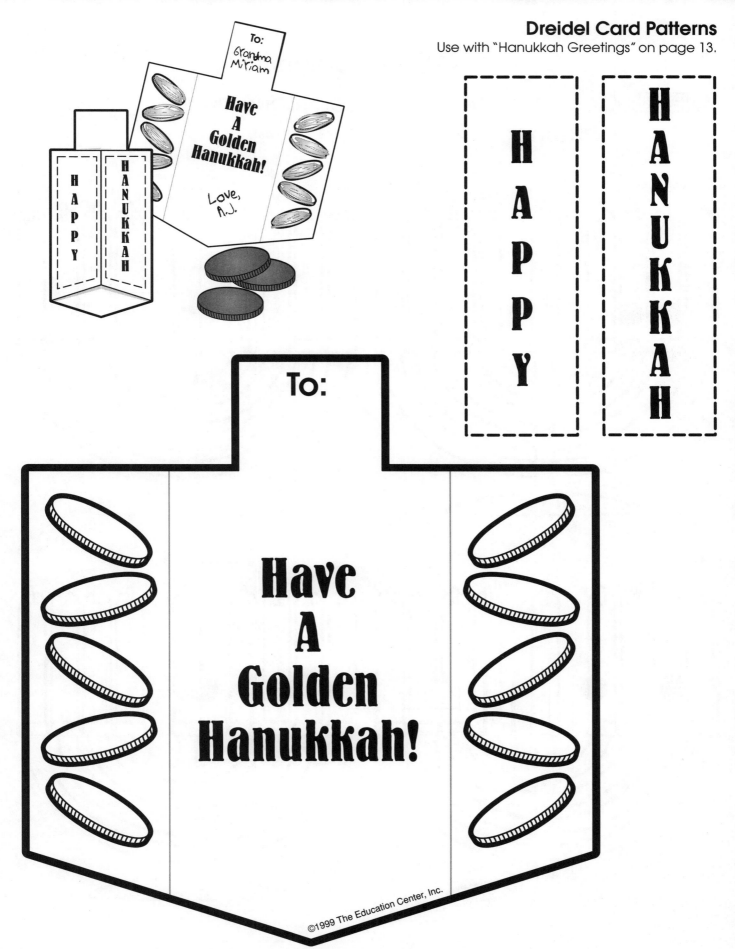

To:

Have
A
Golden
Hanukkah!

HAPPY

HANUKKAH

©1999 The Education Center, Inc.

Candle Colors

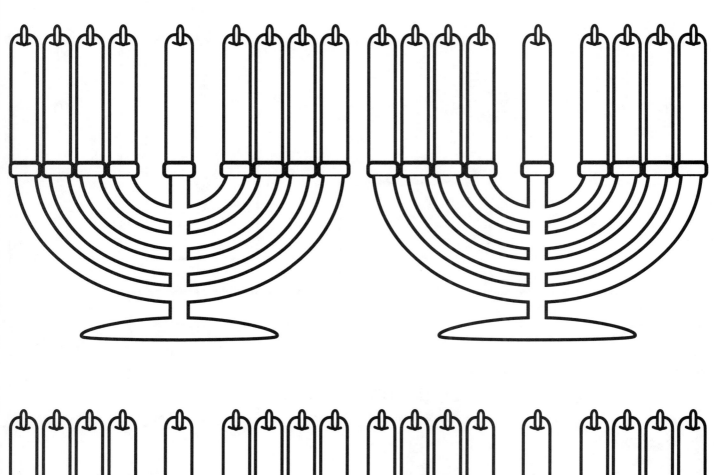 Color the candles in each menorah to create a pattern.

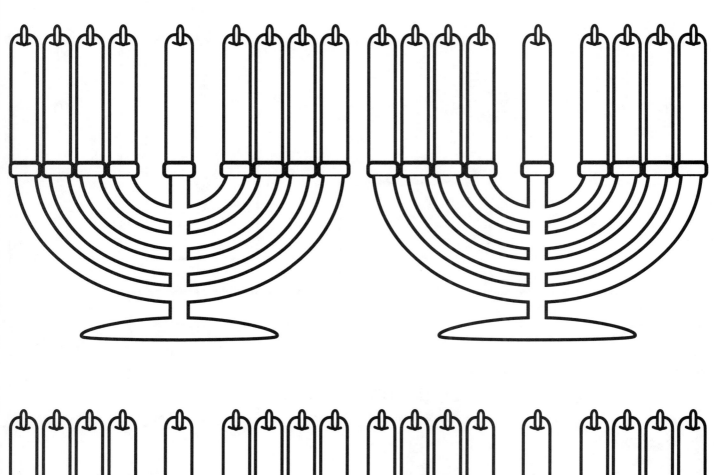

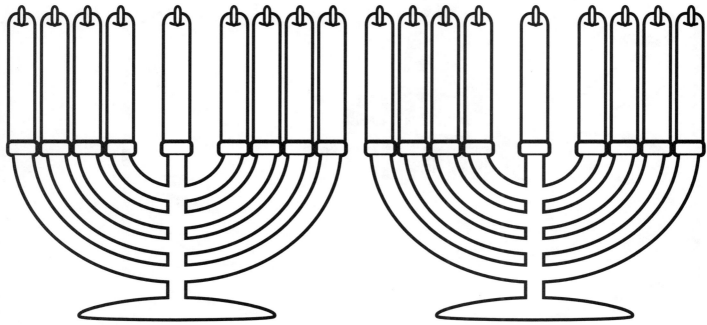

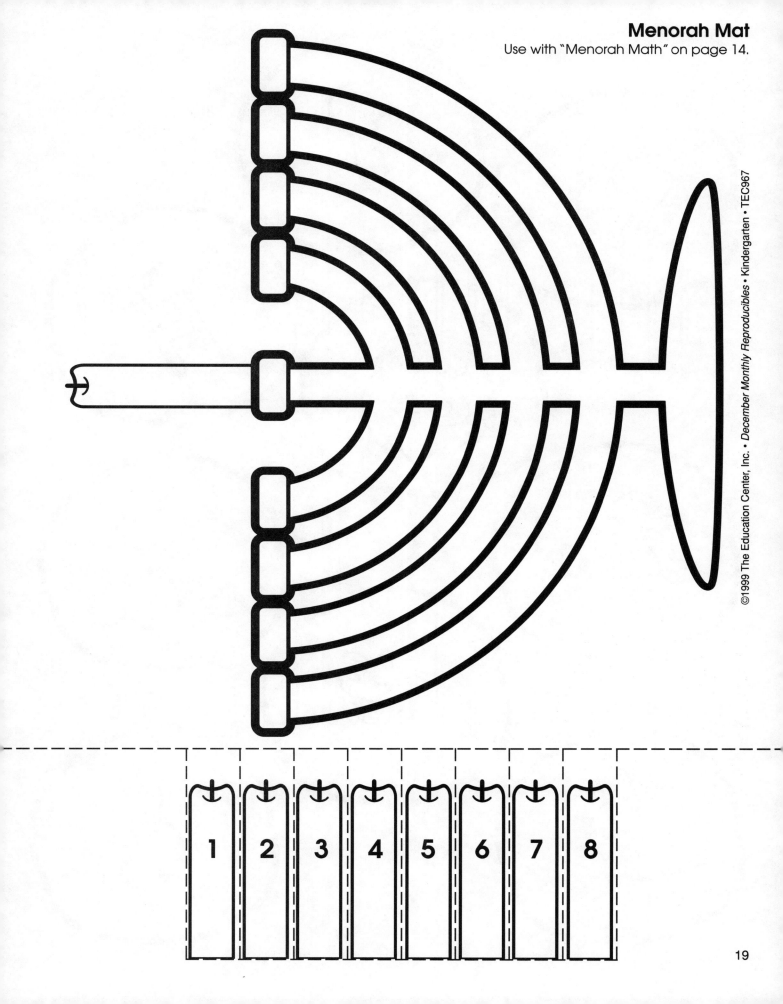

1 2 3 4 5 6 7 8

Latke Patterns
Use with "*L* Is For Latkes" on page 14.

Mmm...Gingerbread!

The reproducibles in this unit focus on a holiday favorite for some sweet and spicy learning opportunities.

Some Delicious Reading

This creative booklet about a mouse and her gingerbread house will certainly satisfy emergent readers' appetites. For each child, duplicate pages 22–26 onto white construction paper. Read through the directions and gather the necessary materials. To make the booklet, have each child color and cut out her pages and pattern pieces, then complete each page according to the following instructions:

Cover: Glue the house plan to the corresponding space on the page. Draw some small cookies and candies in the open space below the house plan. Write your name where indicated.

Page 1: Glue the window to the page where indicated. Glue large sequins or paper dots to the opening in the candy tin and around the windowpanes.

Page 2: Glue the knife blade to the page where indicated. Sponge-paint pink or brown tempera-paint frosting on the page to the right of the mouse. Shake candy sprinkles or small craft beads onto the paint while it is still wet.

Page 3: Glue the cookies to the page where indicated. Decorate each cookie with glitter.

Page 4: Glue the door to the page as indicated so that it can open and shut. Decorate the windows as described for booklet page 1. Decorate the roof cookies as described for booklet page 3.

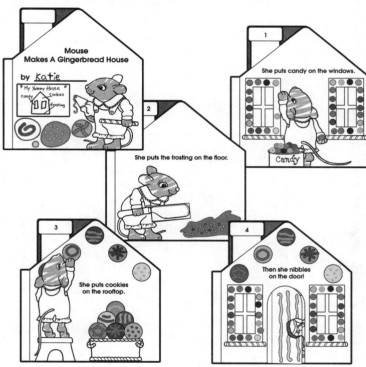

After the paint and glue are dry, help each child sequence her pages behind the cover and staple her booklet together along the left side. Read the booklet aloud several times; then encourage students to practice reading their booklets individually.

A Gingerbread House For Me!

Tempt tiny taste buds with these gingerbread cookie cottages. To prepare, have parents donate a supply of white frosting, sugar wafers, and peppermint sticks as well as a variety of edible decor, such as candy sprinkles, M&M's® candies, and Gummi Savers® candies. Mix up a batch of your favorite gingerbread-cookie dough. Then cut several house-shaped templates from cardboard.

Roll out the dough and help each child cut around a house template with a plastic knife. Place his cookie on a square of aluminum foil labeled with his name. Place all of the foil-backed cookies on a large cookie sheet; then bake and cool as directed. To decorate the gingerbread cottages, each child frosts his cookie, adds half of a sugar wafer for a door and a piece of peppermint stick for a chimney, and then adorns the rest of the house with various candies. Be sure to take photos of the finished products, because they won't last long—chomp, chomp!

Mouse
Makes A Gingerbread House

by _____

My Yummy House
candy
cookies
frosting

Color.

Cut.

Glue.

Draw candy and cookies.

22

1

She puts candy on the windows.

Candy

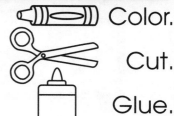 Color.

Cut.

Glue.

Decorate the windows.

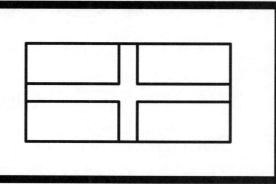

2

She puts the frosting on the floor.

©1999 The Education Center, Inc. • *December Monthly Reproducibles* • Kindergarten • TEC967

 Color.

Cut.

Glue.

Sponge-paint frosting.
Add sprinkles.

3

She puts cookies
on the rooftop.

Color.

Cut.

Glue.

Decorate the cookies.

4

Then she nibbles on the door!

Glue door here.

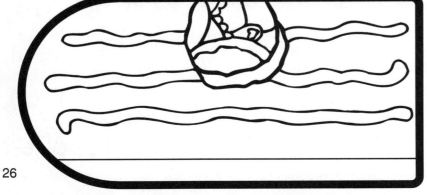

Color.

Cut.

Glue.

Decorate the house.

A Mouse! A Mouse!

Scamper through the curriculum as your youngsters nibble on these mouse-themed learning activities.

The ABCs Of Cheese

The "hole" alphabet is the focus in this activity. Duplicate a class supply of page 29. Direct each child to fill in the missing letters, color the picture, and read the alphabet to a friend. For a fun extension, try to brainstorm a list of cheeses that start with each letter of the alphabet. Let's see: **A**merican, **b**lue, **c**ottage…

Hurry Home!

Quick! The cat is coming! Have your youngsters help the mice on page 30 find their holes. Duplicate a class supply of page 30. Instruct each child to draw a straight line from each mouse to its corresponding home. For ease in checking, have him use a different color of crayon for each line. (The programming on this page has been arranged so that it can be easily masked out and replaced with another skill of your choice.)

HOME SWEET HOME

Nibble, Nibble, Nibble

Send your little critters home with these mousy bags filled with a cheesy afternoon snack. Obtain a class supply of white or brown paper lunch bags and several bags of cheese puffs. Duplicate the patterns on page 31 onto construction paper for each child. To make a mouse bag, a child fills his bag with two cups of cheese puffs. Next he folds the top of the bag in and down as shown to form a triangle. Staple the child's bag closed. Then have him color, cut out, and glue the mouse features and poem to the bag. Encourage him to share the poem and his bag of snacks with his family.

This bag holds a tasty treat,
Something that mice love to eat.
Open the bag, if you please.
Mice aren't the only ones that like cheese!

A Very Merry Mouse

Not a creature is stirring *except* for a mouse in this holiday booklet for your students to make. Read through the following directions and gather the necessary materials. Duplicate a class supply of pages 32–34. Have each child cut apart her pages; then help her complete each page according to these instructions:

Cover: Write your name where indicated. Color the page. Glue a small white pom-pom to the end of the hat.

Page 1: Use a black washable-ink pad and a fine-tipped marker to make a fingerprint mouse in the stocking. Glue on torn pieces of paper to cover the stocking.

Page 2: Use a black washable-ink pad and a fine-tipped marker to make a fingerprint mouse under the tree. Color the page; then glue on sequins to resemble ornaments.

Page 3: Color the page; then use a black washable-ink pad and a fine-tipped marker to make a fingerprint mouse on the present. Tape a piece of curly ribbon (or stick a tiny self-adhesive bow) to the present.

Page 4: Draw your face on the sleeping figure provided. Use a black washable-ink pad and a fine-tipped marker to make a fingerprint mouse beside you on the page. Glue the left edge of a 3 1/2" x 4 1/2" piece of fabric to the page where indicated to resemble a blanket.

When the pages are complete, have the child sequence them behind the cover and staple them together. Practice reading the booklet several times before encouraging your little ones to take the booklets home to share with their families.

Cute As A Button

These friendly mice are just what a busy teacher needs! Duplicate a supply of the mouse patterns on page 34 onto construction paper. Cut out the patterns and use an X-acto® knife to make slits along the dotted lines. Use the open space on the mouse to write a reminder, give praise, or relay any other bit of information to parents. Then fasten a mouse to each student's clothing so that a button becomes the mouse's nose.

Name _____

The ABCs Of Cheese

✏ Write the missing letters.

🖍 Color.

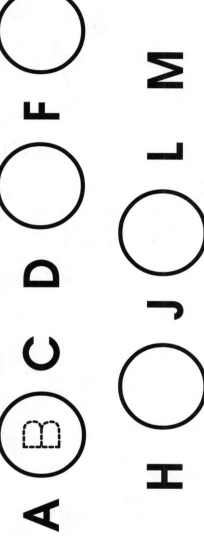

A B C D ○ F ○

H ○ J ○ L M

N ○ ○ Q R ○ T

○ V ○ X ○ ○

Hurry Home!

Draw a line from each mouse to its matching hole.

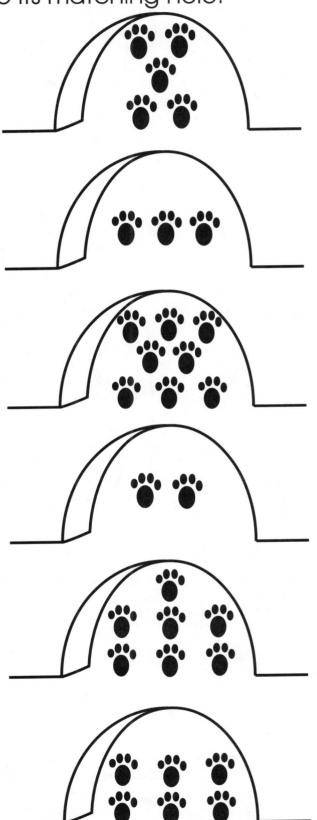

ears

eyes

nose

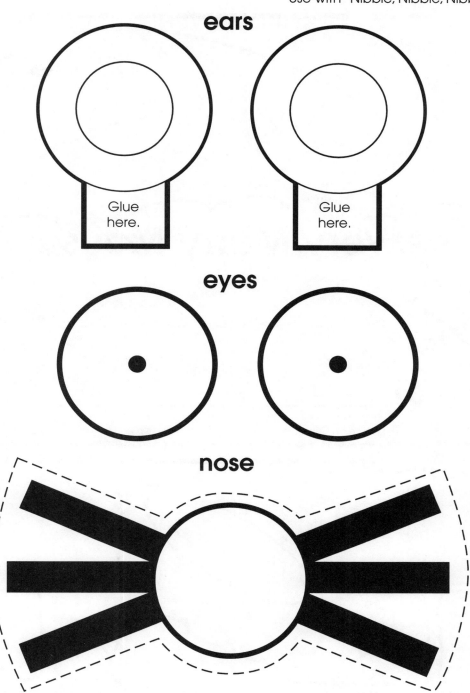

Glue here.

Glue here.

poem

This bag holds a tasty treat,
Something that mice love to eat.
Open the bag, if you please.
Mice aren't the only ones that like cheese!

Booklet Cover And Booklet Page 1

Use with "A Very Merry Mouse" on page 28.

A Very Merry Mouse!

By: _____

Staple here.

The mouse is **in** the stocking.

1

The mouse is **under** the tree.

2

The mouse is **on** the present.

3

Booklet Page 4

Use with "A Very Merry Mouse" on page 28.

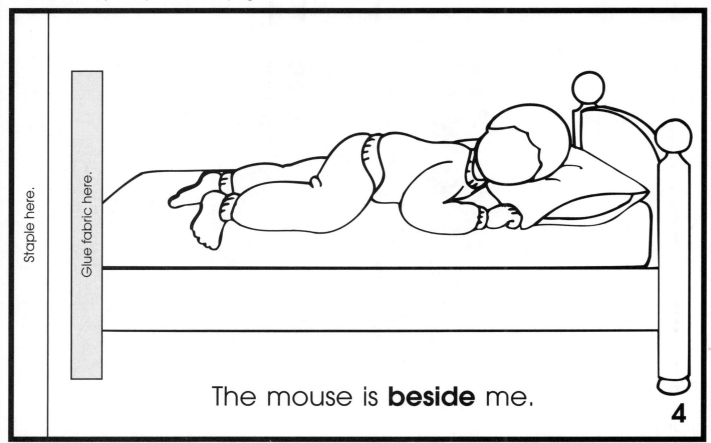

Staple here.

Glue fabric here.

The mouse is **beside** me.

4

Mouse Patterns

Use with "Cute As A Button" on page 28.

MERRY CHRISTMAS!

Introduce your little merrymakers to the sights and sounds of Christmas by enjoying some of these festive holiday learning activities.

Christmas Icons

Reindeer, candy canes, and ornaments? It *must* be Christmas. Here's a game that uses holiday symbols to sharpen youngsters' discrimination and comparison skills. To prepare, cut out an even-numbered supply of colorful gift-box shapes from construction paper (or purchase a package of die-cut calendar markers that resemble gifts). Duplicate the gameboard on page 37 onto tagboard. Color the gameboard; then cut it out and laminate it. Place the gift cutouts in the center of the gameboard. Provide a die and game markers for two players.

To play, each partner takes a turn rolling the die and moving her marker the designated number of spaces. If she lands on a Christmas symbol, she takes a gift. If she lands on any other symbol, her turn is over. When the gift pile is depleted, have youngsters compare their amounts to see who has the *most* gifts. Then, in the spirit of Christmas, encourage them to divide the gifts so that each person has the *same* amount.

Dandy Candy

Your children will be seeing stripes after completing this sweet activity. Give each child a copy of page 41. Have him trace each numeral, then draw the corresponding number of stripes on each piece of candy. Christmas just wouldn't be complete without peppermint!

Ornament Artists

'Tis the season to create beautiful ornaments, but the job is only half done here. Duplicate page 39 for each child. Have her finish drawing the ornament's designs, then color it. If desired, make the copies on construction paper and provide a variety of craft items—such as glitter pens, sequins, and colored glue—for embellishments. Have each child cut out her completed ornament and attach it to a large tree cut from bulletin-board paper. What an ornate display!

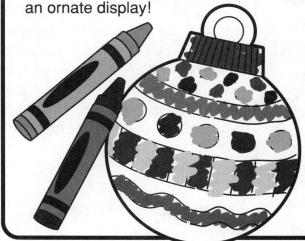

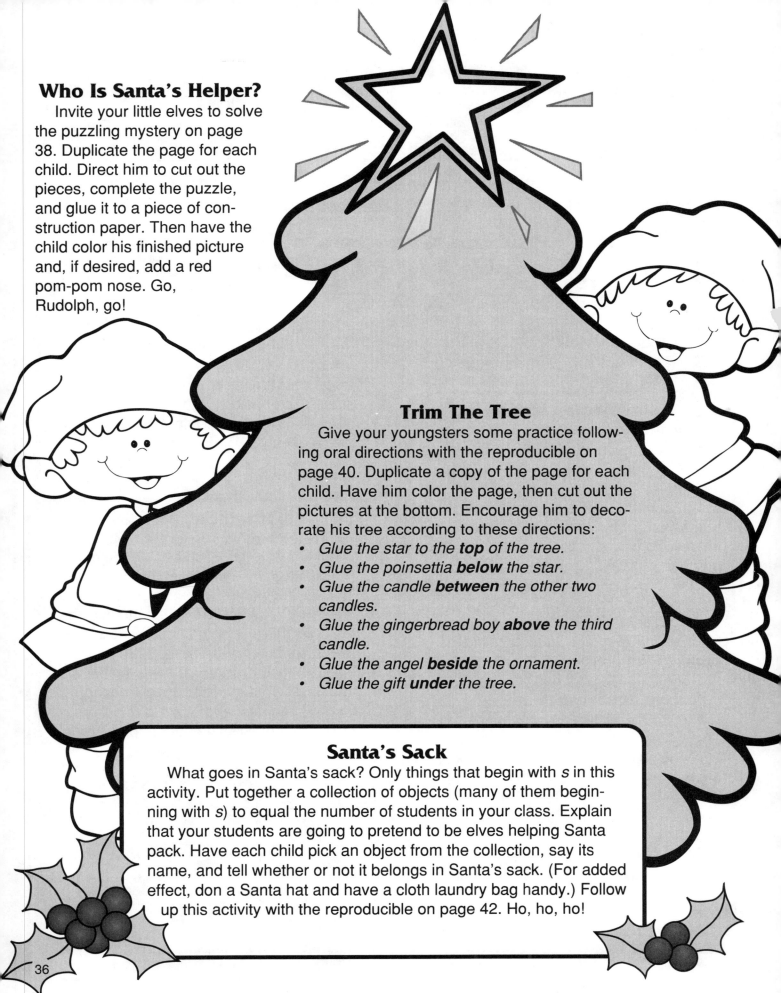

Who Is Santa's Helper?

Invite your little elves to solve the puzzling mystery on page 38. Duplicate the page for each child. Direct him to cut out the pieces, complete the puzzle, and glue it to a piece of construction paper. Then have the child color his finished picture and, if desired, add a red pom-pom nose. Go, Rudolph, go!

Trim The Tree

Give your youngsters some practice following oral directions with the reproducible on page 40. Duplicate a copy of the page for each child. Have him color the page, then cut out the pictures at the bottom. Encourage him to decorate his tree according to these directions:

- *Glue the star to the **top** of the tree.*
- *Glue the poinsettia **below** the star.*
- *Glue the candle **between** the other two candles.*
- *Glue the gingerbread boy **above** the third candle.*
- *Glue the angel **beside** the ornament.*
- *Glue the gift **under** the tree.*

Santa's Sack

What goes in Santa's sack? Only things that begin with *s* in this activity. Put together a collection of objects (many of them beginning with *s*) to equal the number of students in your class. Explain that your students are going to pretend to be elves helping Santa pack. Have each child pick an object from the collection, say its name, and tell whether or not it belongs in Santa's sack. (For added effect, don a Santa hat and have a cloth laundry bag handy.) Follow up this activity with the reproducible on page 42. Ho, ho, ho!

Start

Who Is Santa's Helper?

Ornament Artists

✏️ Draw.
🖍️ Color.

Name _____

Trim The Tree

🖍 Color.

✂️ Cut.

Listen.

Glue.

©1999 The Education Center, Inc. • *December Monthly Reproducibles* • Kindergarten • TEC967

40

Dandy Candy

 Trace the numerals.

Draw red stripes.

6

5

3

7

4

2

Santa's Sack

Color only the objects that begin with *s*.

EVERGREENS EVERYWHERE!

Indoors and out, evergreens are popular at this time of year.
So use them to branch out into learning in a "tree-mendous" way!

Three On A Tree

Like all trees, an evergreen has three basic parts. The *roots* help the tree absorb water and nutrients from the soil. The *trunk* holds up the branches and allows water and food to travel between the roots and the leaves. The *crown* includes the branches and leaves (or needles). Sketch a simple evergreen on your chalkboard; then discuss with students the name and function of each of these parts. Follow up the discussion by having each child complete a copy of page 44.

Evergreen Puppets

Make these adorable puppets for some evergreen dramatics. Duplicate a class supply of the tree puppet patterns on page 45 onto green construction paper. Give each child two precut trees. Have her write her name on one tree shape. Then have her glue two wiggle eyes on the other tree shape and add a red-glitter smile. Provide a variety of white materials—such as white glitter, white sequins, or bits of cotton batting—so each child may add "snow" to her tree. After the glue has dried, staple the two tree shapes together as shown, wedging a bit of crumpled tissue paper between them for a stuffed effect. Then insert a wide craft stick into the trunk and secure it with glue. Teach students the following poem. Then have groups of five use their puppets to perform the poem for the class.

Five little evergreens standing all together.
The first one said, "I love December weather!"
The second one said, "It's going to snow tonight."
The third one said, "Then our Christmas will be white!"
The fourth one said, "Let's look up at the sky."
The fifth one said, "Is that a flake I spy?"
Then down came the snow 'til it covered every tree,
And the five little evergreens shouted out, "YIPPEE!"

Tall, Taller, Tallest

Help students practice size comparisons with the reproducible on page 46. Duplicate the page for each child; then have the child color and cut out her six trees. Direct her to glue the trees in order from shortest to tallest on a 6" x 18" strip of construction paper. Small trees, tall trees—we love *all* trees!

43

Three On A Tree

Color.

Cut.

Glue.

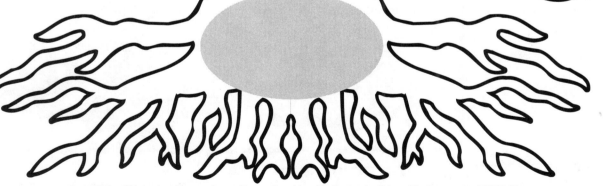

crown

trunk

roots

Puppet Patterns
Use with "Evergreen Puppets" on page 43.

Tree Patterns
Use with "Tall, Taller, Tallest" on page 43.

Yum's The Word!

Give your little ones a recipe for success with these fun cooking-related activities!

Stocking The Pantry

Every good cook has a well-stocked pantry, so give your dramatic-play area a boost with these creative kitchen items. In the center, place a variety of pots and pans, plastic measuring cups and spoons, blank recipe cards, aprons, tablecloths, unbreakable dishes, utensils, oven mitts, empty food boxes (stuffed with paper and taped shut), and interesting gadgets.

For a fun twist, add several things that do not belong in a kitchen, such as blocks, math manipulatives, and playground toys. Invite students to visit the kitchen, decide which items belong there, and remove the items that do not. Then provide your discriminating chefs with copies of page 49 for more classifying practice.

What's For Dinner?

Wonder what's cooking in this puzzling activity? Healthful foods your youngsters put together, of course! Cut the front panels off several food boxes; then cut each panel into a jigsaw puzzle. Store each puzzle in a separate plastic food container. After each child has put together a few of these panel puzzles, give him a tagboard copy of page 50 to make a puzzle of his own to take home. Have the child color the picture as desired. Then instruct him to cut out the puzzle pieces on the heavy lines. Provide a personalized resealable plastic bag for the child to store his puzzle pieces in. Dinner isn't such a puzzle anymore!

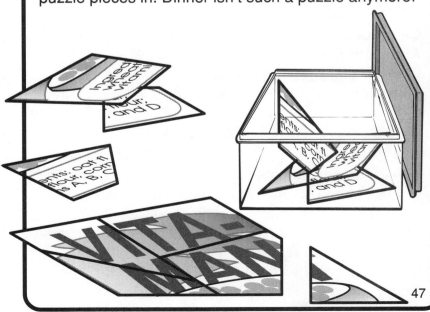

47

Measuring Up

Good cooking requires excellent measuring skills. Provide cupfuls of practice with this activity. Stock your sand table with plastic measuring cups and spoons, and a variety of nonstandard measurement tools, such as drinking cups, whipped-topping containers, and detergent scoops. Instruct each student to experiment with all of the measuring tools. Then give the child a copy of page 51 and a 6" x 18" strip of construction paper. Have her cut out the cups and spoons. Then have her sequence and glue the cups to one side of the strip and the spoons on the other side. Your little chefs will measure up well!

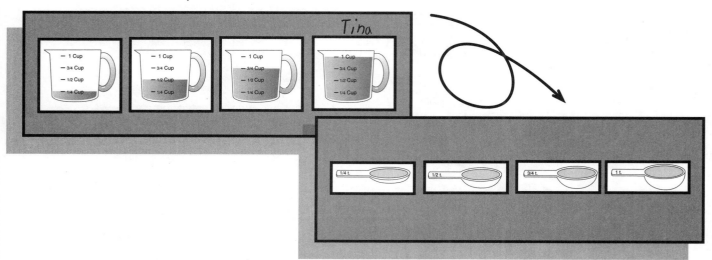

Who Stole The Chef's Spoon?

Who stole the chef's spoon? Not me! Engage youngsters in this name game adapted from "Who Stole The Cookie From The Cookie Jar?" As you teach the following chant, tell each child to listen for her name and then respond during her turn in the chant. For added fun, pass around a wooden spoon and have each child hold it during her turn.

(The leader names one child to start play.)
All: Who stole the spoon from the chef's pot?
All: [Child's name] stole the spoon from the chef's pot!
Child: Who, me?
All: Yes, you!
Child: Couldn't be!
All: Then who?
Child: [Another child's name]
(Repeat as many times as desired.)

Meet The Chef

Invite your little ones to dress for cooking success with these easy-to-make chef hats. Duplicate a class supply of page 52 onto white construction paper. To make a chef's hat, each child personalizes and cuts out a hat pattern, then glues or staples the hat onto a sentence strip. When the glue is dry, staple the headband to fit the child's head. Ooh la la!

48

Name _____

A Crazy Kitchen

🖍 Put an X on each mistake.

🖍 Color.

49

Food Puzzle
Use with "What's For Dinner?" on page 47.

Hat Pattern

Use with "Meet The Chef" on page 48.

Finished Sample

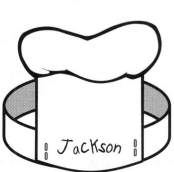

IT'S KWANZAA!

Habari gani? (What's the news?) That's the traditional greeting for Kwanzaa. Use the reproducibles in this unit to help you teach your kindergartners about this African-American cultural holiday, celebrated December 26 through January 1.

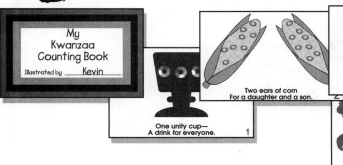

My Kwanzaa Counting Book — Illustrated by Kevin

One unity cup—
A drink for everyone. 1

Two ears of corn
For a daughter and a son. 2

Three different colors
On the bendera I see. 3

Four gifts I made
For my special family. 4

Five fruits to eat,
So juicy and sweet. 5

Six yummy yams
For a tasty treat.

Seven bright candles
In the kinara shine.

Eight pretty stripes
In this mkeka of mine. 8

Nine black-eyed peas
Make my hoppin' John just right. 9

Ten smiling faces
Celebrate Kwanzaa tonight! 10

Count On Kwanzaa

Use the reproducible counting booklet on pages 54–59 for a fun review of the principles and symbols of Kwanzaa. Duplicate a class supply of each page onto white construction paper. Then invite each child to cut apart his booklet pages and illustrate each one following the directions below. Have students work on their booklets over the course of a few sessions, then assemble the booklets once all the pages are completed.

Cover: Color the border with red, green, and black crayons. Write your name on the line.

Page 1: Color the unity cup with a gold or silver crayon. Glue on some sequins.

Page 2: Color the corn. Glue some unpopped popcorn kernels to the cobs.

Page 3: Color the stripes on the flag.

Page 4: Color the gifts. Glue on ribbon, yarn, or pipe-cleaner scraps.

Page 5: Color the fruits and bowl. Glue a strip of rickrack to the bowl.

Page 6: Press a cut sweet potato into a mixture of orange and brown tempera paint; then make six prints on the page.

Page 7: To make candles, glue three red construction-paper strips on the left side of the kinara, three green strips on the right side, and one black strip in the center. Top each candle with a dot of glue and a gold-glitter flame.

Page 8: Glue a 3" x 6" piece of tan construction paper to the page. Glue eight 3 1/2-inch lengths of red yarn across the tan rectangle to make stripes.

Page 9: Glue some uncooked rice and nine dried black-eyed peas to the opening of the dish.

Page 10: Draw a smiling face in each circle.

"Corn-y" Counting

During Kwanzaa, ears of corn—or *muhindi*—are displayed on the table to represent the number of children in the household. Use the corn pattern on page 54 to make your own display showing the number of children in your class. Have each child cut out a yellow construction-paper copy of the pattern, color the husk green, and then write his name on the cob with a black marker. Display the corn on a door or bulletin board and let the counting begin!

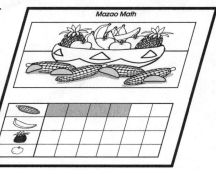

Mazao Math

Mazao are fruits and vegetables displayed on the Kwanzaa table to represent the harvest. Use the reproducible on page 60 to harvest graphing skills! Duplicate the page for each child. Have her count each item and color in the graph. For added fun, give each child ten Runts® candies to use as markers. When the graphing is complete, the ten candies are a treat—yum!

My
Kwanzaa
Counting Book

illustrated by _____

Pattern
Use with " 'Corn-y' Counting" on page 53.

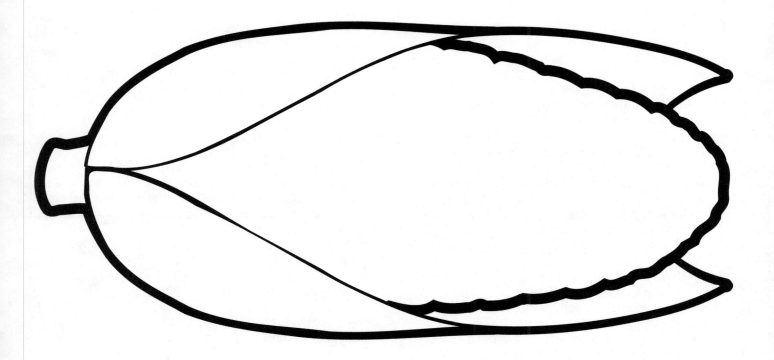

**One unity cup—
A drink for everyone.**

1

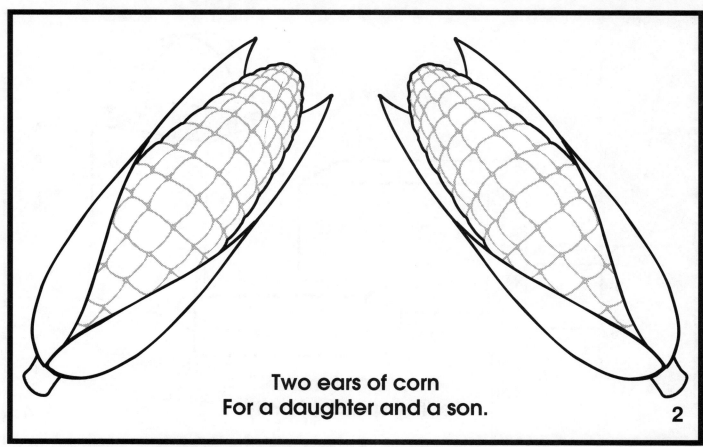

**Two ears of corn
For a daughter and a son.**

2

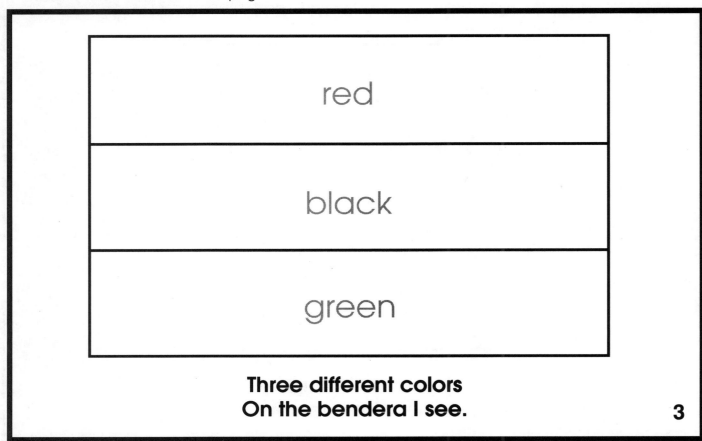

red

black

green

**Three different colors
On the bendera I see.**

3

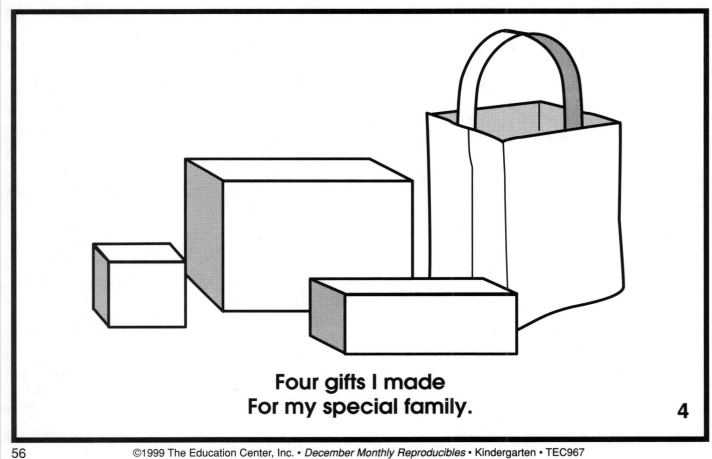

**Four gifts I made
For my special family.**

4

**Five fruits to eat,
So juicy and sweet.**

5

**Six yummy yams
For a tasty treat.**

6

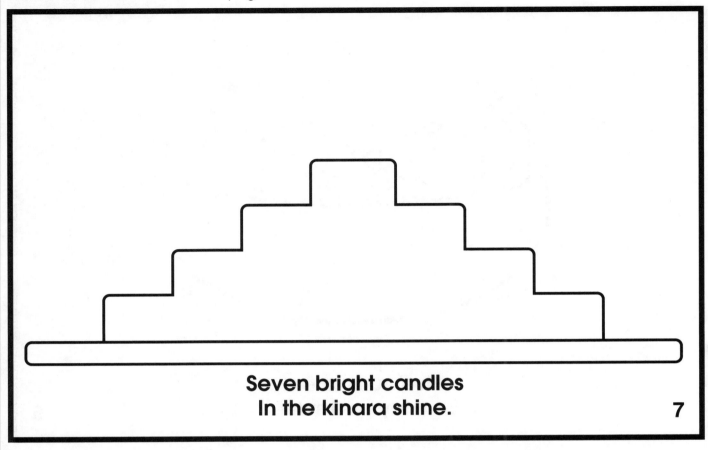

**Seven bright candles
In the kinara shine.**

7

**Eight pretty stripes
In this mkeka of mine.**

8

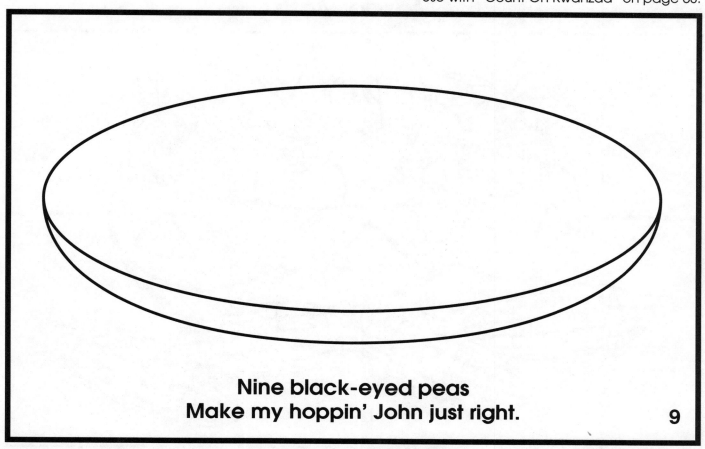

**Nine black-eyed peas
Make my hoppin' John just right.**

9

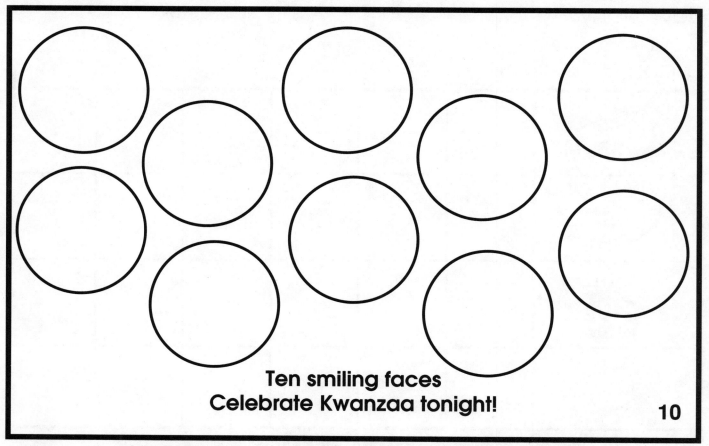

**Ten smiling faces
Celebrate Kwanzaa tonight!**

10

Mazao Math

How many?
Count.
Graph.

	1	2	3	4	5	6
🌽						
🍌						
🍍						
🍎						

LET'S HEAR IT FOR NOISE!

Noise! It's a constant part of our lives, and sometimes there's more than we would prefer. Since we can't beat it, why not join in the fun with these noisy (but productive!) activities?

Items Needed:
wooden spoon and metal saucepan
two wooden blocks
coins in a glass jar
cotton balls in a glass jar
stapler
bell
scissors
coffee mug and metal spoon

Did You Hear Something?

Round up a few familiar noisemakers for some auditory discrimination practice. To prepare, duplicate a class supply of page 62, gather the items listed at the left, and put up a screen to hide these objects from your students' view.

Arrange your little ones around the screened area. Show them each noisemaker and the sound it makes; then hide it from view. Give each child a copy of page 62 and direct his attention to the first row of objects. Instruct him to listen again as you make a sound with one of the pictured noisemakers. Have him circle the corresponding picture on his recording sheet. Complete the rest of the sheet in this same manner. Sounds like fun!

Sound Sorting

Some noises are loud, some are quiet, and some can be both. Create a Venn diagram for each child by programming a large sheet of white construction paper with two large, overlapping ovals. Label one oval "noisy," the other oval "quiet," and the overlapping space "both." Discuss *volume* with students, and ask them what types of things can make both loud and soft noises. Next, provide each child with a copy of page 63. Have her color and cut out the pictures. Instruct the child to sort the pictures and glue each one into the *noisy, both,* or *quiet* category on her diagram. Then encourage her to draw additional items of her choice in the proper spaces. Get ready for some lively discussion about noise!

We've Got Rhythm

Rhythm is an organized pattern of noise, so use this activity to turn random noises into rhythmic patterns. Duplicate a copy of page 64 for each child. Have the child color and cut out the pictures on his sheet. Next, instruct him to create a pattern with the sound pictures, then perform the pattern. After the child has experimented with several different arrangements, have him choose one and glue the corresponding pictures onto a sentence strip. Extend the activity by placing blank copies of page 64 and a supply of sentence strips in a center for students to create more organized noise.

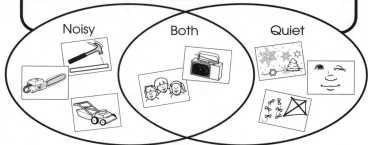

Noisy   Both   Quiet

Did You Hear Something?

 Listen.

Circle to show what made the noise.

  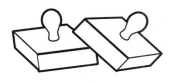 

   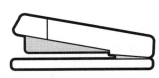

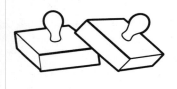   

  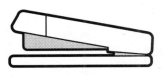 

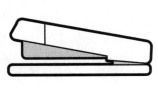   

Pattern Cards

Use with "We've Got Rhythm" on page 61.

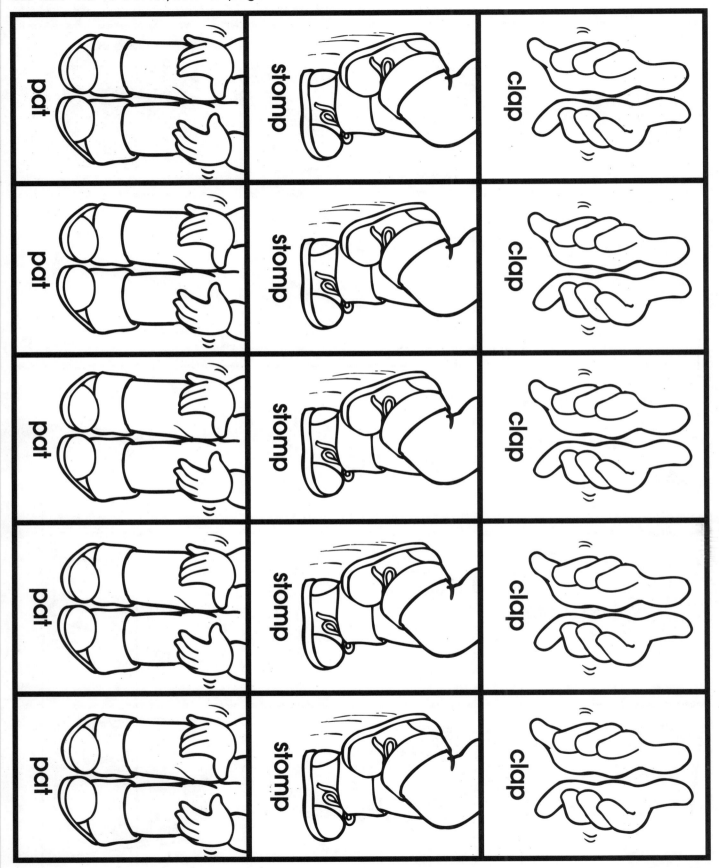